Deliverance

Biblical Truth Simply Explained

Baptism with the Holy Spirit
Jack Hayford

Biblical Meditation
Campbell McAlpine

Blessings and Curses
Derek Prince

Deliverance
Bishop Graham Dow

Forgiveness
John Arnott

The Holy Spirit
Bob Gordon

Prayer
Joyce Huggett

Rejection
Steve Hepden

Spiritual Protection
Lance Lambert

The Trinity
Jack Hayford

Trust
Tom Marshall

Worship
Jack Hayford

Deliverance

Graham Dow

Chosen Books

A Division of Baker Book House Co
Grand Rapids, Michigan 49516

© 2002, 2003, 2004 by Graham Dow

Published in the USA in 2004 by Chosen Books
a division of Baker Book House Company
P.O. Box 6287, Grand Rapids, MI 49516-6287
www.bakerbooks.com

Originally published under the title *Explaining Deliverance* by Sovereign
World Limited of Tonbridge, Kent, England

Printed in the United States of America

Library of Congress Cataloging-in-Publication Data
Dow, Graham.
    Deliverance / Graham Dow.
        p. cm. — (Biblical truth simply explained)
    Includes bibliographical references.
    ISBN 0-8007-9365-X
    1. Exorcism—Textbooks. 2. Exorcism—Biblical teaching—Textbooks.
I. Dow, Graham. Prayer. II. Title. III. Series.

BV873.E8D69 2004
235'.4—dc22

2003055527

Unless otherwise indicated, Scripture quotations are taken from the HOLY
BIBLE, NEW INTERNATIONAL VERSION®. NIV®. Copyright © 1973,
1978, 1984 by International Bible Society. Used by permission of
Zondervan. All rights reserved.

Scripture quotations marked NASB are taken from the NEW AMERICAN
STANDARD BIBLE ®. Copyright © The Lockman Foundation 1960, 1962,
1963, 1968, 1971, 1972, 1973, 1975, 1977, 1995. Used by permission.

Scripture quotations marked KJV are taken from the King James Version of
the Bible.

Notes for Study Leaders

This book is a biblical and practical study of deliverance. The teaching is not just meant to be discussed—it is to be acted on, here and now. Five study questions at the end of each chapter are designed to help members of a study group think about and engage personally with this subject.

As a leader you will need to balance the needs of individuals with those of the whole group. Don't be surprised if different opinions and feelings arise during the study, particularly when answering certain questions. It is wise not to get side-tracked, devoting too much time to one person's thoughts. Instead, enable everyone in the group to share and to respond to the positive message of the book.

This study should take place in an encouraging and receptive atmosphere, where group members feel able to share openly. Encourage group members to read one chapter prior to each meeting and think about the issues in advance. Reviewing the content of the particular chapter at the meeting will refresh everyone's memory and avoid embarrassing those who have not managed to do the "homework."

Praying together and asking for God's help will help each person to take hold of the truths presented. Our hope is that as readers think and pray through the subject of deliverance, they will become freer and more fruitful in all areas of their lives. May God bless you as you study this material yourself and lead others in doing so.

Preface to the Second Edition

This booklet is offered primarily for the increasing number of Christians who are persuaded of the reality of evil spirits and who seek guidance as to how to practice deliverance ministry. For those who need a more detailed explanation, I have addressed the grounds for believing in demons in a separate paper. I also recommend Graham Twelftree's *Christ Triumphant,* an extension of his Nottingham University doctorate on the subject of Jesus the exorcist.

Since I wrote the first edition of this booklet, the former Jesuit priest Francis MacNutt has published *Deliverance from Evil Spirits.* Francis has a wealth of experience in the ministries of healing and deliverance and covers the subject admirably. He deals with whether or not demons really exist, explains how he first became involved with this ministry and gives instruction on how to pray for deliverance.

Some may be concerned that a booklet such as this gives Satan too much attention. I thoroughly sympathize with this view as I have no interest in glorifying Satan. However, in a short booklet on deliverance ministry it is not possible to cover the necessary ground without looking closely at Satan's work.

In this second edition, chapter 4 has been rewritten for the sake of clarity. There is also substantial extra material in chapter 5 to clarify the theological truth that gives a firm basis for the faith necessary to bring about deliverance. Otherwise, the content of the booklet remains much as in the first edition with only minor adjustments.

Graham Dow
Carlisle, 2003

Acknowledgments

I am indebted to those who read the manuscript for the first edition and made many helpful comments. These include Bishop Simon Barrington-Ward, Canon David MacInnes, Audrey Martin-Doyle, Bishop David Pytches, and all the members of the Grove Pastoral Group at the time of my writing the first edition.

I also wish to express my warmest gratitude to the people of Holy Trinity Church, Coventry, England. They lovingly gave me the freedom to share and teach among them and were willing to undertake the journey of taking risks, making mistakes and learning together.

Contents

Foreword

by Simon Barrington-Ward, former Bishop of Coventry

I shall never forget living and ministering in a student hostel at Ibadan University, Nigeria, and spending my first holiday in a Nigerian village. This had a radical impact on my approach to combating evil. I had to learn new ways of praying, preaching and teaching.

I have traveled since in Africa and Asia, staying with people in the churches there, and this has been a significant learning experience. Many non-Western cultures are keenly aware of the powers of evil at work in the daily details of life. Moreover, books like the psychiatrist M. Scott Peck's *People of the Lie: The Hope for Healing Human Evil* are beginning to seriously examine the phenomenon of evil in our own society.

When I first came across Graham Dow's approach to these issues here in the midst of our Western culture, I felt uncertain quite how to respond. At the very least I was impressed enough, as I trust readers of this book will be, to want to look carefully and discover what I had to learn.

While I still do not feel entirely at home with this subject, I have already gained a greater understanding of evil and deliverance from Graham's approach to it, as I do from so many other aspects of his ministry. I would therefore urge the most skeptical reader to suspend disbelief and explore seriously what Graham is opening up to us. There are lessons for us all.

One of the most important of these is the way in which Graham demystifies "evil spirits," even if he refuses to demythologize them. His treatment of them so reduces them in scale and significance as to disclose them to be a manageable nuisance and nothing more. This takes a great deal of the sting out of the fears and fantasies of any who have attributed too much to such causes. It reduces the exotic significance of the occult and the bizarre, so fashionable in many quarters today.

Graham's work shows us that in this area, as in so many, "perfect love casts out fear" (1 John 4:18). A sane faith in God's love in Christ delivers us from every kind of evil within and without, in whatever form it may take. It is this sense of peace and balance in Graham's whole approach that gives it its own weight. I am grateful to him both for his ministry and for this book.

1

Introduction and Examples

This booklet is offered as one minister's experience in the field of the ministry of deliverance from evil spirits. It is the result of a journey. Whereas some years ago I believed that the presence of evil spirits in a person in the Western world was rare, I now believe that such spirits are widespread. But in my judgment, most of them are not powerful and can be dealt with straightforwardly. They easily pass undetected in a culture that does not believe in their existence.

I take the idea of the commonplace presence of evil spirits to be in agreement with the worldview of reality indicated in the gospels of Matthew, Mark and Luke. In these books, the driving out of evil spirits was treated as routine. It was practiced in close association with a healing ministry, as the Kingdom of God was announced by Jesus.

In our twenty-first century I would like to see the ministry of deliverance take its place as a normally routine and unspectacular ministry, alongside prayer for healing, confession, counseling and medical and psychiatric help, each form of knowledge making its own contribution to the healing process. It is only the so-called developed Western countries that have difficulty with belief in evil spirits. The majority of the world is quite used to understanding them as a valid part of reality. The question in many other cultures is not "Do demons exist?" but "Who has power over them?"

The dean of a Chinese theological college, when visiting the diocese of Coventry in a Mission in Partnership exercise in 1988, roared with laughter when I told him that most English clergy do not believe in evil spirits. We should be open to the possibility that the rest of the world is correct in its perception of the way things are.

I am sometimes asked, "Why should we accept a two thousand-year-old worldview today?" The answer I give is that the New Testament view of spiritual reality should at least be considered without prejudice. Perhaps it makes better sense of what we experience than the interpretations commonly offered by our society.

In my experience, even among Christians, this open and unprejudiced hearing is rarely allowed. This suggests that we are afraid of the possibility of evil spirits—they are unthinkable to us. Or perhaps their theoretical existence is acceptable, provided that they are only rarely encountered! Behind this denial there is a far-reaching cultural prejudice against both the supernatural and whatever is outside our human control. We do not like the idea of unseen spiritual powers influencing our lives.

We are glad to believe in God insofar as He provides us with an explanation for the world and help in time of trouble. Many people are less disposed to the belief that they are accountable to Him. Most people believe in a supernatural God to the extent that it suits them. And it is even harder to accept that the Spirit of God may act powerfully with a tangible presence, like breath or wind.

On the other hand, people constantly have experiences of transcendence that challenge their awareness of the Spirit of God. For some it is a beautiful sunset; for others it is listening to music, or walking through a cathedral, or perhaps the awe of seeing a newborn baby. Somehow people know that there is Someone who is greater than human life, and they are aware of His presence. However, many today have no language for speaking of these encounters with the majesty of God.

On the dark side, people also experience the sense of evil— for example, in certain rooms or buildings, or when face to face with a certain person. Again, our culture gives no language with which to speak of the spiritual forces they are encountering. The very idea of the devil or demons is often ridiculed.

Our society has been bankrupt in its understanding of spiritual things, but there are signs that this is changing. The

Christian Church is learning again to welcome the Holy Spirit's power as a vibrant reality in daily experience, and so also it is becoming more open to the possibility of evil spirits. In short, we are regaining our belief in spiritual power.

The Church has a long tradition of consecrating its church buildings. Many ministers are also asked to bless houses from time to time and even sometimes to deal with a "presence of evil" in a house. People intuitively sense that there is such a thing as the sacred presence of God but that there can also be unholy presences.

Since spiritual reality is not open to empirical observation, arguments for the existence of spirits are difficult to confirm or deny. We can neither prove nor falsify the existence of evil spirits, any more than we can the existence of God or of angels. If we are going to know the truth, it will only be through revelation from God, through both the Scriptures and the natural order. This revelation can then be confirmed through our experience and in the consistency of reason.

"But how can a loving God allow a realm of invisible spirits to affect us?" is the sort of question still uppermost in some people's minds. This is actually a key to understanding the whole problem of evil in God's world. To believe in rebellious, fallen angels (Jude 6; Revelation 12:9) is not, in principle, more difficult than to believe in human beings' free will to rebel and sin.

God, in His wisdom, has allowed the existence of a world in which we have been given the choice between right and wrong. Consequently, we are able to do immense harm to one another. Yet we can also learn to love and care for one another and choose what is right. Moreover, as Christians we have the power of Christ to resist evil, both in ourselves and others.

Some Examples of Deliverance

Linda

Linda is a strong and stable person with no indication of psychological disturbance, yet she discovered as she grew up that she had unsought occult powers. She had pre-knowledge of when certain people were going to die, which numbers had won raffles and when certain people were coming in her direction although they were still out of sight. She was attracted to books on witchcraft, and as she read them, she knew that she had the power to do the things described in the books. She also experienced strong, irrational opposition within her to Christian leaders, even to the point of wanting to harm them.

We discerned the presence of evil spirits she had inherited from the practice of witchcraft in earlier generations of her family. Deliverance was accomplished gradually over several years. It took this amount of time partly because of my inexperience, but more particularly because of Linda's need to totally renounce the powers she had inherited and bring her will completely into submission to Jesus Christ. She did not find this easy. Her occult powers had been with her throughout her entire life and to discard them seemed to be to lose something of her own self.

Tony

I met Tony when he was a student. While I was praying for emotional healing and security in Christ, I affirmed that he was God's child and that his home was in heaven. Quite suddenly his voice said, "No, it is not." It was a demonic spirit speaking from within him. Marked physical manifestations of the presence of a spirit repeatedly followed in his eyes, face and body.

Several areas of sin were renounced, step by step, including sinful sexual behavior and his interest in films such as *The Exorcist,* but the spirit stubbornly refused to depart. Several prayer sessions were held. Eventually Tony was willing to face the possibility of inherited powers and admitted to seeing violent tendencies in his father. A murdering power was discerned, and when challenged the spirit said, "You've found me."

Deliverance was slow for two reasons. First, there was a problem in discerning the nature and origin of the leading spirit. Tony was reluctant at first to discuss the clues to inherited spirits that could be found in his parents' behavior. Second, I began to see that although he could speak easily of a faith in Christ, the reality behind this faith was shallow and there was a lack of deep conviction and repentance. The time over which deliverance took place enabled a far deeper faith to be developed.

Frances

Frances became a Christian while studying for a professional qualification. However, after she got married, a strange desire to despise and verbally attack her husband became apparent, a desire that she did not wish to have.

I knew that her mother was a dominant, controlling person who had once gone for three years without speaking to her husband. I also knew that there was usually one member of the family with whom the mother was not communicating. This indicated that Frances had inherited a spirit that was now attacking her relationship with her husband.

As we prayed, we became aware of witchcraft rituals and devil worship in Frances' ancestry. In our final ministry time, through spiritual gifts, Frances and the two people praying for her independently received pictures of a black stone, a ritual chalice and the words *devil worship*. It transpired that her grandmother had practiced fortune-telling. Renouncing these ancestral acts proved difficult for her, but she eventually managed to do so, calling, "Jesus, help me."

As we served holy Communion to her, something in her desired to attack me, but finally her deliverance was accomplished and the spirits were thrown out. The irrational desire to attack her husband was completely gone.

Some years later she wrote:

> *Since then my life has been much the better. We have a very good marriage. My relationship with my mother is quite different, and no longer do I fear being "the one out of favor." Everything is much improved, including my own self-image.*

Mary

Mary came forward at a conference for prayer in response to this word from the Lord: "There is someone who is longing to find hope for the future." Her husband had died nearly ten years earlier, and she had become increasingly desperate. Even from her childhood she had little enthusiasm for life and had almost looked forward to death.

Without knowing anything about Mary, through the Holy Spirit I discerned a spirit of abandonment. This coincided exactly with how she had felt in the months before the conference. We believe that this spirit entered her father when he was an eighteen-year-old recruit in the First World War and, like thousands of others, felt completely abandoned during and after the Battle of the Somme. This led him to have a major breakdown after the war, and eventually the spirit of abandonment passed to his daughter.

Mary was set free from the spirit of abandonment and from a spirit of death. She wrote:

> *I still cannot get over how different I feel. I feel a new person, and I believe in one sense I am! I feel loved and accepted by God more than ever before.*

Seeing some of the same marks in one of her children, she has subsequently met with others in prayer and sought to bring a similar release to her son.

Please note the names of the people in these examples have been changed. Also, although two of these particular examples involved the practice of witchcraft in previous generations, this does not mean that witchcraft is always involved.

Study questions:

1. What is your initial response to the idea of evil spirits and deliverance? To what extent do you think this is conditioned by your cultural expectations?
2. Is it easier to believe in some aspects of the supernatural world than in others—for example, is the concept of the Holy Spirit easier to accept than that of the devil?
3. Why does deliverance sometimes take time, as in the case of Tony?
4. How can past experiences and family ancestry affect our spiritual state?
5. Do the stories of Linda, Tony, Frances and Mary remind you of any issues in your own life?

2

Deliverance Ministry in the New Testament

It is important to see how deliverance ministry is presented in the Bible, particularly in the gospels and the book of Acts.

Dealing with Spirits Was Routine Ministry for the Disciples

Far from being told by Jesus that dealing with evil spirits was a ministry that required special skills, the disciples were given straightforward instructions to cast out spirits and heal every disease (Matthew 10:1; Mark 6:7, 13). Both deliverance and healing were seen as an integral part of announcing the arrival of the Kingdom of God (Matthew 9:35). "When Jesus had called the Twelve together, he gave them power and authority to drive out all demons and to cure diseases, and he sent them out to preach the kingdom of God and to heal the sick" (Luke 9:1–2).

Jesus did not say, "If you come across an evil spirit, take great care; report to Me before proceeding." The impression, rather, was given that dealing with evil spirits was as common and routine as dealing with sickness (though not to be confused with sickness). It follows then that the ministry of deliverance can be handled by all Christian disciples who are acting with Christ's authority.

Deliverance Is Distinct from Healing

Jesus did not treat all disorders as the result of evil spirits, and treated apparently similar conditions as on some occasions requiring deliverance and on other occasions not.

Contrary to what has been argued elsewhere, the writers of the New Testament did not interpret disorders in demonic terms simply because such was the prevailing perception in their day. While a dumb and blind person was cured by deliverance (Matthew 12:22–23) and a dumb person similarly so (Matthew 9:32–33), laying on of hands—with no hint of deliverance from spirits—was used for both a dumb man (Mark 7:32–37) and a blind man (Mark 8:22–25).

It was, in fact, quite well known in the ancient world that mental disorders could rise from organic or psychological causes, and these were not necessarily attributed to demonic causes. Examples of this can be found in Herodotus' *History* (2.173.4; 6.84.1) and Hippocrates' *On the Sacred Disease* (chapters 1, 17, 18). In *Christ Triumphant,* Graham Twelftree refers to the critical stance of Josephus, Philo and Lucian toward supernatural claims.[1]

Demons and Evil Spirits Are the Same Thing

In Mark 6:7–13 it appears that the *evil* (in the Greek, literally *unclean*) spirits over whom the Twelve were given authority were the same as the demons they cast out on their mission. Similarly, the spirit in the Syro-Phoenician woman's daughter is called both an "evil" spirit (Mark 7:25) and a "demon" (verse 29).

We also see this in Matthew's gospel: "When evening came, many who were demon-possessed [Greek: *demonized*] were brought to him, and he drove out the spirits with a word and healed all the sick" (Matthew 8:16).

Spirits Are Invisible Supernatural Forces

Both the Old Testament Hebrew and New Testament Greek words used for *spirit* are the same as those used for *breath* and *wind,* indicating real but invisible power. The Holy Spirit is compared to wind (John 3:8). When Jesus gave His Spirit to the disciples, He breathed on them (John 20:22). Similarly, I find it helpful to think of most evil spirits as rather like bad breath in a person!

Throughout the gospels there is no hint of spirits which are good, other than the Holy Spirit, and there is no indication that Jesus allowed spirits to remain in a person when the Kingdom of God drew near. The presence of spirits is best described as "having" spirits; it is unhelpful to speak of people's being "possessed" by a spirit or demon.

Various descriptions of demons used in the gospels and the book of Acts include:

- *to be demonized* (found in many references; poorly translated as *possessed by a demon*)
- *having a spirit* (a dumb spirit: "a spirit that has robbed him of speech," Mark 9:17; "an evil spirit," Mark 7:25; "evil spirits," Acts 19:13; "a spirit by which [the person] predicted the future," Acts 16:16; "a demon," Luke 4:33)
- *a man with an unclean spirit* (Mark 1:23, NASB)
- *being seized by the demon* (Luke 8:29)
- *many demons had gone into him* (Luke 8:30)
- *a spirit that seizes him* (Mark 9:18)
- *troubled by evil spirits* (Luke 6:18)
- *tormented by evil spirits* (Acts 5:16)

The words *demonized* or *having a demon* do not necessarily imply that the person has been taken over by the demon, a concept which we understand by the word *possessed*. In my judgment we should speak of people's *having spirits* rather than *being possessed*.

Demons, or Spirits, Are of Varied Strength

The variety of words used to describe demonic involvement indicates the varied degrees of affliction that can be caused by these spirits. The usual word for a *demon* in the New Testament is the diminutive word *daimonion,* which means something that has either divine or demon-like attributes. In the popular understanding of Jesus' day, these were not always considered to be evil, nor were they necessarily thought to be particularly powerful. Their existence was simply accepted as part of the way things were.

The stronger word *daimon* is used in Matthew's account of

the man whose spirits claimed to be "Legion" (Mark 5:9). The diversity of the words used for *demons* suggests that spirits were thought to exist in varying strengths. In Luke's account the trouble afflicting the man is variously described as *demons, the demon* and *the evil spirit* (Luke 8:27–36). This shift between singular and plural suggests several spirits, with one in particular being key to the deliverance.

Driving Out Spirits Is Part of Liberating People from Satan's Rule

The gospels and the book of Acts present Jesus' coming to earth as a battle in which the rule of God has come to set people free from the rule of God's enemy, Satan. Jesus Himself said, "If I drive out demons by the finger of God, then the kingdom of God has come to you" (Luke 11:20), and "Should not this woman, a daughter of Abraham, whom Satan has kept bound for eighteen long years, be set free on the Sabbath day from what bound her?" (Luke 13:16).

In Acts 10:38 we read, "God anointed Jesus of Nazareth with the Holy Spirit and power, and . . . he went around doing good and healing all who were under the power of the devil, because God was with him."

Although Satan is in no way the equal of God, at the present time he is the "prince of this world" (John 12:31; 14:30; 16:11). Because of that, "your enemy the devil prowls around like a roaring lion looking for someone to devour" (1 Peter 5:8). Satan was actually in a position to offer Jesus all the kingdoms of the world (Matthew 4:8–9).

Luke 11:14–23 portrays the ministry of deliverance as a struggle for dominance between two strong men. Since it is a power struggle, it is not surprising to read that Jesus used more than one command to release the afflicted man (Luke 8:29, 31). The disciples on at least one occasion failed to effect deliverance at all (Matthew 17:14–16).

The good news is that Jesus secured final victory at the cross (John 12:31–32). At every level He sets people free to enjoy the peaceful rule of God. Sins are forgiven, bodies are healed, relationships are put right, righteousness and justice spring up and evil spirits are evicted as the Kingdom of God arrives. Paul declared that Jesus had sent him to the Gentiles "to open their eyes and turn them from darkness to light, and from the power of Satan to God" (Acts 26:18).

Jesus Threw Out the Spirits with a Command

Graham Twelftree writes:

> *From data both within and outside the New Testament there is no doubt that Jesus was an exorcist—a very successful exorcist. Jesus never used the formula "I exorcise you by the Spirit of God." Instead he said "I command you [to come out . . .]" showing clearly that he thought he was acting on his own authority while being endowed with the Holy, eschatological Spirit.*[2]

The use of the Greek word *ekballo,* meaning "I drive out" (Luke 11:20), confirms that with His own authority, Jesus confronted an enemy who was frustrating the purpose of God in His people. On occasions, shouting, screaming or strong physical movements accompanied the departure of the spirits (Mark 1:26; 9:26; Luke 4:33–36, 41).

The Disciples Commanded Spirits in the Name of Jesus

"Lord, even the demons submit to us in your name."
Luke 10:17

"In the name of Jesus Christ I command you to come out of her!"
Acts 16:18

The gospels and the book of Acts show us that the disciples conducted their healing ministry as they had seen it modeled by Jesus, except for the additional invocation of His name (Acts 3:6; 9:34).

Graham Twelftree convincingly shows in *Christ Triumphant* that Luke wrote his two-volume work (the gospel of Luke and the book of Acts) to show the close parallels between the Holy Spirit at work through Jesus and the Holy Spirit at work through the apostles. The continuity is clear.[3] Throughout the ages, it is the same ministry of Jesus, who began to do and teach things during His life on earth and continues to do so through His Church (Acts 1:1–2).

This means that we can read the accounts of Jesus' ministry as a model for our own practice rather than just as the wonderful works of the divine Son of God.

We Must Contend against a Range of Unseen Spiritual Powers

Other parts of the New Testament give us further indications of the spiritual reality that lies behind the presence of evil spirits. Paul wrote:

> Put on the full armor of God so that you can take your stand against the devil's schemes. For our struggle is not against flesh and blood, but against the rulers [*archas*—hierarchies], against the authorities [*exousias*], against the powers of this dark world [*kosmokratores*—world controllers] and against the spiritual forces of evil in the heavenly realms.
>
> Ephesians 6:11–12

The battleground for the Christian is not primarily against human factors in opposition to Christian life, but against a range of unseen evil spiritual powers. The words used in this passage give clues that these powers operate in a hierarchical pattern descending from Satan, and seek to exercise controlling authority over human life. This view relates to the Jewish belief at the time of Jesus that individual nations were associated with specific angelic powers in the heavens.

Further light is shed on this idea in the book of Revelation. Satan is described with the imagery of heads, horns and crowns (Revelation 12:3). In the following chapter, similar horns, heads and crowns are ascribed to a beast to which Satan gives "his throne and great authority" (Revelation 13:1–2). This beast rules with power, persecuting Christians, and is understood by many scholars to be the Roman Empire, and in particular the emperor Nero, coming to life again.[4]

Here the truth is expressed that spiritual powers of evil operate through human affairs, including the rise and fall of nations. A second demonic beast follows the first, supporting its authority (Revelation 13:11–12), and is later called the false prophet (Revelation 16:13). This imagery shows Satan's placing his authority onto human institutions or leaders when they embrace evil. While the interpretation of such symbolism is never a straightforward matter, here is further biblical evidence to support the view that unseen spiritual powers of evil are a reality in our fallen world.

Study questions:

1. How is deliverance similar to healing in the gospel accounts? How are they seen as distinct and different?
2. What language can we use to describe evil spirits and their activity?
3. What was the significance of Jesus' driving out evil spirits?
4. How did the disciples follow Jesus' example in deliverance ministry?
5. Do you consider unseen powers of evil to be a reality that you must deal with?

Notes

1. Graham Twelftree, *Christ Triumphant: Exorcism Then and Now* (London: Hodder and Stoughton, 1984).
2. Ibid., p. 96.
3. Ibid., p. 110.
4. G. B. Caird, *The Revelation of St. John the Divine* (London: Black, 1966), p. 162.

3

The New Testament View and Our Understanding Today

It is often argued that Jesus was a man of His time and therefore interpreted sickness in terms of evil spirits. However, we have already seen that Jesus exercised discrimination, treating similar conditions as requiring deliverance on some occasions but on others not.

Further, Jesus showed Himself well able to disagree with other prevailing interpretations of His day. For example, He declared that sickness was not necessarily due to sin (John 9:1–3); that children were to be treated with significant status in the Kingdom of God (Mark 10:13–16); and that forgiveness could be pronounced with God's authority by His anointed representatives (Mark 2:5–11; John 20:23).

It is true that the understanding of the world's being affected by Satan or demons is a late Jewish doctrine developed in the Hellenistic period. But so also is the doctrine of life after death that Jesus taught and to which we cling eagerly! It is impossible to separate Jesus' references to Satan and demons from His understanding of His own mission, proclaiming the arrival of the rule of God and breaking the enemy's hold over the world.

No one has yet offered any adequate criteria by which we might decide which aspects of Jesus' teaching we should set aside as culturally determined and which we should not. The accepted ideas of our own culture in deciding what is plausible (right or wrong) are inadequate grounds for dismissing those of the New Testament.

Personal Experience

I have personally picked up evil spirits in a way that taught me of their reality. Some years ago I prayed with a woman to set her free from a fear of cancer. I did so with an air of self-confidence rather than a sense of dependence upon God. It so happened that at this time my wife's father was dying of cancer. From the moment I prayed that prayer, I could not control my thoughts about cancer. It was as if my mind simply "took off." I had to put all thoughts of my father-in-law out of my mind because I could no longer handle such thoughts rationally. When I asked someone with experience to cast the spirit out of me, I was fine, but I would not have believed this possible had it not happened to me.

On another occasion I picked up a spirit that made me choke when taking holy Communion. Neither of these spirits was very powerful, but they hindered my Christian life and I am certainly very glad to be free of them.

"Does It Matter If We Believe in Evil Spirits?"

If we fail to believe in evil spirits, we will be unable to correctly diagnose the cause of a problem when an evil spirit is present. This commonly leads to failure to release the person from the power of that spirit. I doubt that the people described in chapter 1 would have been helped by any other professional discipline.

Of course, there are dangers in holding such beliefs. Just as those who spend a lot of time in the hospital see a great range of human disorders and are liable to forget the amazing healing abilities of the human body, so a belief in the wide-spread presence of evil spirits can make one forget the power of God that can drive their presence away. Confession of sin, prayer and worship, the sacraments of the Church and obedience to God all play a vital part in protecting believers from spiritual attack and in setting them free when an attack takes place.

It is as difficult to attest to the existence of angels as of demons. Yet angels are mentioned three hundred times in the Bible. They are described as "ministering spirits sent to serve those who will inherit salvation" (Hebrews 1:14). Angels have a long and glorious tradition in Christian worship, theology and art. But if we choose to doubt the existence of evil spirits, we must realize that the case for the existence of angels is no stronger.

"Surely a Christian Cannot Have an Evil Spirit?"

From my own experience I am quite certain that a Christian can have an evil spirit. Perhaps the incorrect use of the word *possessed* has been the trouble here. We know that Christians are united with Christ at the center of their beings, but sin still remains in us. It no longer *rules* us but it *presses in on* us. According to James, when we allow ourselves to be enticed by an evil desire, it "gives birth to sin; and sin, when it is full-grown, gives birth to death" (James 1:15).

In a similar way, Christians who have an evil spirit find it pressing in on them; it influences their will, just as their sinful thoughts and desires affect their will to do what is right. The influence may only appear on certain occasions. I have heard the presence of a spirit likened to the malaria parasite; that is, it seems as if the disorder it creates only erupts at certain times, when the person has lowered immunity.

The Need for Care and Good Advice

While much of the world is convinced that evil spirits are real, this is not the case in Western culture. More recently, much attention has been called to the possibility of spiritual abuse in a variety of ways; so in a culture unsympathetic toward the model of deliverance, mistakes are heavily punished.

Our society is quick to attach blame and is becoming more litigious. In part, this is the result of our losing the sense of God's providence over all things. He is no longer regarded as the first point of help in a difficulty: the One who allowed the situation to happen and to whom we must turn for help. If God is out of the picture, when disaster happens people have no alternative to blaming themselves other than to blame others.

For these reasons, extra care needs to be taken in prayer for deliverance. Here are some guidelines:

- Do nothing that even remotely violates a person's dignity.
- Have other witnesses present.
- Proceed slowly, securing the person's full agreement for what seems to be the most appropriate way to pray.
- When a person is under professional care, work with the professionals concerned.
- Ask a doctor to advise and, if any difficulty is expected, to be present.
- Follow carefully the guidelines for such ministry issued by your local and national church.

Deliverance Should Be in Partnership with Other Ministries

I am not saying that deliverance ministry is the be-all and end-all of healing ministry, or even that it should be the dominant ministry practice. My hope is that it will take a routine place in partnership with other ministries. I look forward to the day when Christian ministers, physicians and psychiatrists can learn together in mutual trust when and how deliverance prayer can be effective. But this requires openness to explore the truth of deliverance ministry as a means of healing.

Study questions:
1. How should we decide which aspects of Jesus' teaching to accept in our day and age?
2. What difference does it make if we believe in evil spirits?
3. How can a Christian have an evil spirit?
4. In what ways should deliverance be practiced responsibly and "in partnership" with other ministries?
5. Are you open to understanding more about deliverance and its place in the Church?

4

Clues to the Presence
of Evil Spirits

I offer this chapter cautiously, but on the basis of 25 years of experience in the deliverance ministry. It is offered as a guide and not as an exhaustive or authoritative treatment of the subject. With that in mind, here are some clues to bear in mind when considering whether or not evil spirits are present. Some of the descriptions may indicate evil spirits on some occasions, but not others. Some may be completely mistaken.

There is a danger in "seeing spirits everywhere." However, I am prepared to take this risk if it opens up new possibilities for effective ministry. In this unfamiliar area, our understanding is very limited, and we have much to learn.

Evil Spirits Live in the Realm of Darkness

Evil spirits live in the realm of sin, of rebellion against God. Only when there is room in a person for such darkness do the spirits have any right of entry. Therefore, persistent sin, deliberately doing what is not pleasing to God, is an invitation to the powers of darkness to enter. Their nature is to create disorder and to ruin human lives: They can cause or reinforce any kind of disaster.

A spirit may be identified by the particular disorder to which it relates. Some evil spirits have names, for example, "a spirit of false gods."

Three Primary Kinds of Sin

1. Our Own Sin

Spirits enter a person through common areas of sin such as violence, occult practice, sexual sin and false worship. They also come through deeply embedded wrong attitudes such as anger, hate, bitterness or unforgiveness. The sin may be knowingly committed, or it may be committed in ignorance. A person may not realize that an action or attitude is *sin*, as, for example, with some occult practices, with fear or with a sense of rejection.

2. Sin Committed against Us

God has created us to be people who live together in community. We can, therefore, affect one another deeply by our words and actions. If we believe the cruel words people say to us, even slightly, that act of belief may give that negative wish or statement a degree of power in our lives. This is a kind of curse: The words are given power over us by a spirit.

Another example of a spirit's entering through sin committed against us occurs in an abusive situation such as rape, violence or other forms of dominance. Fear can offer an entry point for an evil spirit.

3. Sin of Previous Generations

It should not surprise us that spiritual powers, both good and evil, travel from one generation to another. We are beings created to be full of God's Spirit. As with every other part of our nature, this inheritance is passed on to our children. This is not a problem for Christians who take responsibility to make sure nothing evil is passed on to their children.

It may be necessary to seek the ministry of deliverance ourselves or to seek wise and gentle prayer for our children if we sense that something evil has been passed on. But the good news is that the Holy Spirit's positive presence also passes to the next generation!

Since there is little awareness in Western churches of the reality of evil spirits and the churches have lost the art of deliverance, spirits have been passed down family lines for many generations, and their unholy presence has remained in certain locations where serious evil occurred in past generations.

Common Entry Points for Evil Spirits

False Worship

All worship reaching out to transcendent beings or powers involves the spirit realm. There is no other channel that links earth and heaven. Whenever prayers and worship are offered that are not in accordance with the truth of God and Jesus Christ, a link is made with spirits of untruth and their presence is invited. Unfortunately, this is not widely realized.

Other Religions

Paul said to the pagan Athenians that God purposed that people would seek Him in different ways (Acts 17:26–27). But since God has now revealed Himself in the person of His Son, the one true Lord, He commands people everywhere to repent (Acts 17:30).

Other world religions bear many statements about God and human destiny that do not agree with Christian truth. A person's confession of these statements in prayers and religious acts can open the door to the spirits of these religions.

It is also well known that astrology and other occult practices play a major part in several Eastern religions, indicating the association of these religions with the realm of evil spirits. Whenever prayers are said that are not spoken "in truth," evil spirits may be present.

It may be that the early Christian Church had a wiser understanding of the presence of evil than we do in our own day. The early third-century document *Apostolic Tradition*, found in the liturgies of Hippolytus, records that all baptism candidates from that time took part in prayers for deliverance from evil spirits.[1] This would be a strange thing to do if conversion to Christ was all that was needed to bring deliverance from the presence of evil. It seems that the early Christians knew that new believers could bring darkness with them from other religions.

Cults

Modern-day cults, which deny that Jesus is the true God and died for our sins, carry spirits of deceit. Freemasonry, for example, eliminates Jesus from its prayers and gives God the name *Jah-Bul-On* (a combination of the name *Yahweh* with the pagan deities Baal and Osiris). Its Emulation Ritual states that "by square conduct, level steps and upright intentions we hope to ascend to those immortal mansions whence all goodness emanates."[2] This is seeking salvation by morality, not by faith in the cross of Jesus Christ. The secrecy and unholy vows of Freemasonry all indicate its deception. I have once entered a Masonic temple and what was there did not agree with Jesus Christ in me.

Occult Practices

The word *occult* means "hidden." Occult practices, in general, seek knowledge through hidden powers either to find guidance, bring about healing or curse another person. At its most serious level, any past or present involvement in practices claiming to worship or serve the devil will certainly indicate the presence of evil spirits. Considerable psychological disorder is also likely.

It is important to note when a person shows an attraction to occult practices such as witchcraft, spiritualism, fortune-telling and horoscopes, or to occult books, or shows an attraction to those who practice these things. This probably indicates the presence of evil spirits. Darkness seeks out darkness.

The presence of occult spirits is indicated also by superhuman strength or ability, or by inexplicable knowledge other than that which clearly glorifies God. Such knowledge is often called "second sight." This is sometimes a difficult area to discern since occult experiences of knowledge are counterfeit opposites of true words of knowledge from the Holy Spirit.

Occult practices are common in some societies. Writing as a Scot myself, I have become aware, through in-depth prayer ministry, that some with Scottish ancestry may need deliverance from the residual power of clan warfare and its atrocities in past generations. My suspicion is that most so-called "second sight" indicates more serious evil in previous generations, such as curses with violence. Although the evil practice of the past may have since been discarded, its power may not have been fully broken.

This is another example of the way that evil spiritual power can travel through the generations until it is dealt with. "Second sight" is a kind of residual of spiritual power. I have met people who were born with powers of foreknowledge that they never sought and yet that they felt gave them power over others. (See the example of Linda in chapter 1.)

Some people view psychic powers as morally neutral, capable of being used for good or evil. The use of the word *psychic* in this context is unfortunate because, according to the Bible, the *psyche,* or *soul,* is a good and created aspect of our humanity. Through the psyche, we have the ability to share in human relationships and open ourselves to God. The word *psychic* as it is used today, however, concerns itself with hidden spiritual powers which are likely the work of evil spirits, unless they are clearly operating in obedience to Jesus Christ and His Holy Spirit.

Some occult activities such as Ouija boards are commonly considered harmless, but it is foolish to play the devil's games, even for fun. Just as those who come to church for a "laugh" may be touched by the Spirit of God, conversely it can be so with activities that call upon spiritual powers that are not of God.

A woman came to see me who had committed her life to Christ many years earlier but who had never had any sense of God's presence. I realized that something was blocking the Holy Spirit's ministry to her. The clue came when she shared that her father was of dogmatic religious opinions but also was hooked on horror films. In the name of Jesus, I released her from the bondage she had inherited from her father and from whatever evil or occult practice lay behind it in previous generations. The presence of God came to her within minutes of this prayer.

This example shows the need to recover the routine ministry, given by Jesus to His disciples, of casting out spirits. Inherited spirits should be dealt with whenever a person becomes a Christian.

Sin and Wrong Attitudes

Serious and deliberate personal sin is always likely to allow entry to evil spirits. Some common entry points are through sins of abortion, deceit, pornography, wrong sexual relationships, unwholesome sexual practices and self-harm.

Wrong attitudes may have very understandable causes. But to hold on to such an attitude rather than repent and seek God's forgiveness is to take an attitude completely contrary to the teachings of Scripture. Here are some examples:

- "For if you forgive men when they sin against you, your heavenly Father will also forgive you. But if you do not forgive men their sins, your Father will not forgive your sins" (Matthew 6:14–15).

- "But now you must rid yourselves of all such things as these: anger, rage, malice, slander, and filthy language from your lips. Do not lie to each other, since you have taken off your old self with its practices" (Colossians 3:8–9).

- " 'In your anger do not sin': Do not let the sun go down while you are still angry, and do not give the devil a foothold" (Ephesians 4:26–27).

- "Do not repay evil for evil or insult with insult, but with blessing, because to this you were called so that you may inherit a blessing" (1 Peter 3:9).

- "See to it that no one misses the grace of God and that no bitter root grows up to cause trouble and defile many" (Hebrews 12:15).

Where wrong attitudes of bitterness, unforgiveness, anger and hatred are held in our hearts, they are an invitation to a demonic spirit. As we know, such attitudes are all too common, bringing darkness in both families and churches.

One of the best routes to good health is to make sure that there is no one whom we have not fully forgiven. Wrong attitudes, especially when accompanied by an evil spirit, give rise to much illness. Sadly, people seek treatment for their bodily illness without attending to their spiritual disease.

Traumatic Events and Oppression

I have already mentioned violence and rape and their poten-
tial to give entry to evil spirits. Other traumatic events that
can also cause this include war, becoming a refugee, serious
fires or accidents, bereavements and sexual abuse.

The emotions of shock and pain run deep and can make the
human spirit vulnerable to an evil spirit that comes to
reinforce the pattern of brokenness. The ground of entry for
the spirit is the fear, shock or despair. While these responses
are very understandable, they are not God's perfect will and
therefore can bring darkness.

The history of trauma is more pronounced in some nation-
alities or communities than in others. For example, I have
found that deliverance prayer is important for some who have
ancestors who were involved in mining. There is a history of
ruthless exploitation, terrible working conditions and pit
accidents plunging families and entire communities into
terrible grief. A measure of stubbornness and hardness—also
present in the perpetrators—has often developed in reaction
to what happened to the victim.

Oppressive behavior takes many forms, all of which violate
the dignity of another person or community. Attitudes of
condemnation or rejection, for example, have power to affect
us deeply. Finland is a nation which has been invaded by
Russia 53 times, and the consequential sense of hurt and
oppression in some of its people can open the door to
darkness. This is why a nation's history is important in
relation to the presence of evil.

I used to work in an area of London where many church
members were originally from the West Indies. They brought
with them a background of West African voodoo and the evil
practices of witch doctors. In addition, there was a history of
slavery, which seriously affected models of behavior for both
men and women. When most of the population turned to
Christ, the churches lacked the understanding and skill to deal
with the spirits coming down the generations from past evil.
Even among committed Christian people I observed very
strange behavior that I believe can be traced to their troubled
history.

I am increasingly convinced that the spiritual hold related

to such past events must be dealt with, not only in individuals but also at corporate levels. Families, towns, churches and nations, for example, can all be affected. The story of a community is important in the sight of Jesus Christ as the letters to the seven churches make clear (Revelation 1–3).

Ruling Spirits

In the Old Testament four areas of sin are specified as bringing the land into pollution. They include:

* Idolatry (Jeremiah 3:1; 16:18)
* Bloodshed (Numbers 35:33)
* Occult practice (Deuteronomy 18:9–12)
* Sexual immorality (Leviticus 18:1–30)

It seems that serious sin can give evil some degree of ruling presence in a place. This will continue through the years and down the generations until it is dealt with.

Attention needs to be given to these powers and their effect on a house or family, a town or city, an organization, community, church or nation. Spirits which have gained a presence in a particular location are often called "territorial spirits." They can seriously block the progress of the Gospel in that location. Unlocking the history that has given rise to their presence is one of the recent insights in the work of evangelism.

Study questions:

1. What is the significance of sin in relation to evil spirits?
2. How can the sin of others open us to evil powers?
3. What practices and events are common entry points for evil spirits?
4. How can evil spirits be connected with places and families?
5. Is there any way in which your own sin or the sin of others could have provided an entryway for evil in your life?

Notes

1. Gregory Dix, *The Treatise on the Apostolic Tradition of St. Hippolytus of Rome, Bishop and Martyr* (London: Alban Press, 1992).
2. Malcolm C. Duncan, *Duncan's Masonic Ritual and Monitor* (David McKay, 1986).

5

Discerning Evil Spirits

Outward Manifestations

The knowledge that someone is involved in any occult practice alerts us immediately to the probable presence of spirits contrary to Jesus Christ. Here are some other outward signs of the presence of evil spirits.

Reaction against Jesus

Demons will not say that Jesus Christ has come in the flesh on earth (1 John 4:2–3) or that Jesus is Lord (1 Corinthians 12:3). By contrast, they will curse Jesus or deny Him.

It must not be supposed that every person with an evil spirit will be unable to confess that Jesus Christ is Lord and incarnate. It is the spirit which denies the truth, not the person. The believer, through the presence of the Holy Spirit, will usually be able to confess Christ, although some difficulty may be experienced especially if the evil spirit is powerful. However, when people show pronounced difficulty in accepting the foundational doctrines of Jesus as taught by the Church, it is possible that a spirit within them is affecting their ability to receive basic truths. This can shed light on difficulties a person may have, for example, in a confirmation or baptism class.

In addition to cursing or denying Jesus, demons resist the victory of the cross. In saying "Get behind me, Satan!" (Mark 8:33), Jesus recognized that it was not just Peter's human desires that were challenging His journey to the cross. Demons show a hostile and violent reaction in the face of the cross because it was there that they were defeated. One

Christian leader I know recognized that she had a spirit when her lip curled as her minister used the cross on the altar to bring deliverance to another person.

Reaction against Worship, Prayer and Holy Things

Demons react against the worship of God. Clues to their presence can be found in a person's feelings of restlessness or body movements during prayer or worship that seem to be in opposition to, rather than in harmony with, the Spirit.

It is not uncommon to find people who have a reaction against Communion services and cannot explain why. This may indicate an evil spirit. Breaking Communion vessels, defacing Bibles and churches, and blasphemy are more blatant signs.

An irrational dislike of God's ministers, or a feeling of being persecuted by them, may be a sign of an unholy spirit. Conversely, it is a sign of an evil spirit if a person is drawn instinctively to people who have occult connections.

Direct Obstruction of the Work of God

The girl with a spirit of divination obstructed the work of God (Acts 16:16–18). Even though she was apparently speaking the truth, Paul was disturbed by her behavior and commanded the spirit to come out of her. Spirits in people who encountered Jesus called out His name in an attempt to challenge His authority and actually gain power over Him (Mark 1:23–27; 5:7).

I have observed the presence of spirits in mockery, inappropriate laughter, compulsive talking and other distractions during times of ministry. Spirits within people will stir up irrational opposition to godly people or projects, often for no apparent reason. They will inexplicably and repeatedly spoil relationships involving unsuspecting Christians.

If we believe with Paul that our real struggle is not with human factors but with hidden spiritual powers (Ephesians 6:12), then it is helpful before any church council or similar meeting, worship service or counseling session, to use our Christian authority to forbid any disturbance by enemy spirits. I have found it effective in my personal prayers for any such meeting (i.e., prayers not made publicly) to forbid

Satan or his spirits to speak through anyone. I then entrust the meeting firmly to the sole direction of the Holy Spirit and this is where I concentrate my prayers. We must not give Satan or his spirits undue attention; we address them only to rebuke them.

Paranormal Phenomena

In my judgment certain phenomena, such as "haunted" houses and inexplicable movements of objects, doors and windows, indicate spirits affecting the house. My experience suggests that the spirit powers operating may relate primarily either to the place or to the people living there. In either case sin, past or present, must be confessed and renounced, and prayer must be made for deliverance from the spirits in both the person and the place.

Blatant Evil or Immoral Practice

Since deliberate and serious sin opens the door to the entry of spirits, the knowledge of evil practices in someone's life is a fairly sure guide.

A Person's Appearance

On several occasions I have recognized the presence of a spirit in a person's face, looking at his or her countenance with my natural sight. I see the face as being obviously not as God wants it to be. This is different from pain, which can also often be seen in people's faces, but rather a distortion of what I believe to be the person's true countenance.

This indication calls for great care lest normal fear or a similar emotion be attributed to a spirit. It is possible, however, to see evil in a person's eyes; a false smile can be another indication.

The repeated choice of black, for example in clothing or color of car, can in some cases be signs of occult influences. Markedly unrestful color schemes or patterns for dress or house décor are another clue.

Reaction to a Command for the Spirit to Make Itself Known

Christians who need to know of the presence, or otherwise, of a spirit in a person they are counseling may command any spirit present in the name of Jesus Christ to make its presence known. Clear indications are then quite frequently received, for example, through involuntary body movements or pain.

Illnesses and Disorders That Do Not Yield to Treatment
I once experienced a spirit-driven sickness as a mild stomach disorder. Unlike a normal stomach "bug," this condition appeared to have no lifespan and did not follow the usual pattern for an infection. Since the condition started after an encounter in which I thought I had disobeyed God, I suspected that I had picked up a spirit and asked someone with discernment to pray for me. They discerned what it was and released me. The stomach condition was immediately cured.

I have known a case where deafness was brought on by a spirit. I was not expecting any such cause but as soon as I put my fingers gently in the person's ears and prayed for healing there was an immediate manifestation of demons.

It is not easy to discern when a mental illness is affected by the presence of a spirit. I prayed for a woman who had been diagnosed a year earlier with clinical depression. Treatment was making little headway. Looking at her countenance I sensed the need for deliverance, so I explored her story. As a missionary in Nepal she had watched a witchcraft ceremony involving the killing of a cockerel. I addressed these spirits and her body shook as they left. There were also spirits relating to rape and a dominant grandparent. She says that all has been well since the time of prayer.

I am certainly not saying that all disease is caused by a spirit. It is when the normal treatments do not yield the expected results that there is reason to look for another explanation.

Clues from a Person's Present Experience and Attitudes

In the following examples, the presence of a spirit can be indicated by what a person shares about his or her experience.

Persistent Experience of Inner Darkness
This may include spiritual confusion, willful pursuing of heretical beliefs, difficulty in receiving basic Christian truth

and/or persistent blocking of commitment to Jesus. It must be discerned whether these experiences are normal doubts, or whether there is a spirit causing them.

> The god of this age has blinded the minds of unbelievers, so that they cannot see the light of the gospel of the glory of Christ, who is the image of God.
>
> 2 Corinthians 4:4

Marked Blockages in Normal Personality or Spiritual Development
Some people become emotionally stuck in childhood, as parental attitudes prevent them from growing up. A "spirit of a little child" holds them. They are then unable to grow satisfactorily through normal learning experiences into adult behavior. In a similar way, when someone does not seem to grow spiritually through the normal channels of the Word, sacraments and prayer, there may be a spirit blocking this development.

Immovable Bondage to Temptation and Sin
This occurs when real attempts at repentance appear to make no impression on the problems. These may involve the areas of sexual lust, deviant sexual practices (possibly including both oral and anal sex), criticism, unbelief, unforgiveness, bitterness, anger and deceit.

Irrational Fears or Phobias
These do not respond to a person's facing up to them and seeking to overcome them.

Overwhelming Guilt and Self-Condemnation
Satan is the accuser and his accusations bring condemnation, while the conviction of the Holy Spirit leads to repentance and cleansing. John tells us that if our hearts condemn us, the Spirit of God gives us assurance and sets our hearts at rest in His presence (1 John 3:19–24).

A Strong Sense of the Presence of Dead Relatives
If this is a spirit, and not just the wishful thinking of the bereaved person, then opinions differ as to whether or not it is

the actual spirit of the person that for some reason (usually death in disturbing circumstances) has not reached its final destination. If this is the case, a simple committal of the person's spirit to the mercy of God and to Christ will bring freedom. Alternatively, however, the sense of the presence of the dead may be due to an evil spirit that was attached to the dead person and is now seeking to transfer its power. This experience is a common one, and I have come to the view that either explanation may be correct.

Other conditions of disorder in family members of the deceased can be related to the unquiet discarnate spirits of dead relatives.[1] Release is often found to occur through a celebration of holy Communion with the "family tree" placed on the altar. I have personally found this to bring marked release in some cases. However, since faith and Christ's authority are what is needed for effective deliverance, I believe that equally effective results are obtained by prayer that commands release from any spirit presence associated with the dead relative.

A Sense of Fatalism
This attitude presents itself as "what will be, will be." It is strangely common and is a satanic lie that suggests that what will happen to us is already fixed. The plan of God for our lives is reshaped daily in the light of our response to Him. If we believe something is inevitable, we give it power and can even allow disaster into our lives. It is far better to hold only to God's promises as things that are certain to happen.

Addiction
The abuse of drugs, alcohol, smoking, gambling, eating or any other compulsive activity can have a spiritual component. These are widespread but serious.

Anorexia
I believe that anorexia usually involves a destructive spirit, especially since its recovery rate is only about fifty percent. As with many conditions that have their roots in prenatal or childhood rejection, insecurity or bad relationships, there is a great need for the emotional healing of hurts and relationships.

While deliverance may well be part of this ministry, emotional healing is fundamental. When those who have caused the hurt have been forgiven (this should be spoken out loud) and wrong attitudes of resentment or hatred confessed, healing often comes, and the spirits leave because they no longer have any right to be there.

I have learned the hard way that the prayer of deliverance with anorexic people needs great care. It is important to work with a person's consultant or doctor. When the body has suffered a severe loss of weight, it may not physically be able to cope with the rush of power from the Holy Spirit and whatever impact this has on the body chemistry. On one occasion someone who seemed restful and quiet in the hospital bed when I prayed for her, suddenly went into a trance and, for a brief period, failed to recognize members of her family. In God's goodness, she made a full recovery, but what happened took me by surprise and, understandably, gave me difficulty with the hospital staff.

Case Histories

Careful questions about a person's history can provide important clues to the presence of evil spirits. These uncover areas that the person might not think to share unless asked. It is important to inquire about a person's relatives and ancestry as well as about themselves.

The following topics are of particular significance to note in the person or his or her relatives.

- *Any occult practice.* Since spirits travel down inheritance channels until they are driven out, occult experiences of parents, grandparents or other relatives are important clues.
- *Experiences of evil,* such as in rooms or buildings, or in shaking someone's hand, or in unexpectedly seeing faces. Such experiences are quite common.
- *Striking cases of disease* or patterns of disorder repeating down the generations. Some people are "accident prone" to such an extent that it gives rise to suspicion about the

involvement of spirits. See the example of Frances in chapter 1.

- *The community (or national) history* into which the person was born and brought up.

- *Traumatic experiences.*

- *Experience of rejection,* from the start of pregnancy in the womb, to being placed for adoption, in childhood, or later on.

- *Miscarriage or abortion.* In the case of an attempted abortion, spirits of rejection, murder and death are likely. There is a view that a spirit joined to a child who was lost (whether due to a miscarriage or an abortion) can transfer to the next pregnancy and enter the next child. Whatever the explanation, prayer to release someone from the spirit of the preceding "child" seems to be effective.

- *Involvement in religious cults or sects* that deny that Jesus is the true God and died for our sins. There are similar dangers from the practice of transcendental meditation and some forms of yoga in which the mind is opened to influences that are not identified as Jesus and the Holy Spirit of God.

- *Dysfunctional or oppressive family features* or internalized attitudes. One example might be domination, usually by a parent or grandparent. This can allow entry to spirits of control. The rejection of women (misogyny) is another significant feature of some families.

- *Use of certain alternative medicines,* such as homeopathy or acupuncture. It is when these treatments are associated with an unspecified life force or an astrological pattern that the danger comes. This involves openness to spiritual powers other than the Holy Spirit of God.

I emphasize again that these are only clues to possible spirit presence. It should not be assumed that these circumstances always indicate the presence of spirits.

Discernment by Spiritual Gifts

Those who are learning to receive indications from God through the mind, the imagination, the body or indeed any of the senses will be shown the presence of spirits through these varied ways in which the Spirit communicates. Through a very clear dream God once showed me that a particular person was under a curse. As well as seeing spirits in the countenance of people, I have on one occasion seen a demon in the form of a strikingly white death mask covering someone's face. Clearly this was not apparent to other people or the person concerned would have been rushed to the hospital.

It is possible to learn both to hear God's voice (usually in our thoughts rather than aloud) and to see what His Spirit shows us. The first step is to believe that this is not only possible, but likely! The life of Jesus and the book of Acts are full of examples of God's direct communication of knowledge or guidance to His servants.

There often remains a degree of uncertainty about the presence of a spirit. This should be accepted as a common-place aspect of warfare—just as in a battle where there may remain uncertainty about the enemy's whereabouts.

In a society that is unsettled at the thought that spirits might exist at all, this lack of certainty can be difficult to handle, so many advise that spirits should only be diagnosed with great caution and as a last resort. In societies that are more relaxed about the possibility of evil spirits and where it is recognized that most of them are not very powerful, such advice is less necessary.

Study questions:
1. What kind of activity or involvement alerts us immediately to the probable presence of spirits contrary to Jesus Christ?
2. What other outward signs indicate possible spirit activity? Do any of these surprise you?
3. What aspects of the case histories cited give clues to the likelihood of evil spirits?

4. How might we discern the presence of spirits through spiritual gifts?

5. Are you aware of anything in your own life or that of your family members that may be connected with an unholy spirit?

Note

1. See Dr. Kenneth McAll, *A Guide To Healing The Family Tree* (Santa Barbara: Queenship Publishing Co., 1997).

6

Driving Out Evil Spirits

Jesus continues His work through us, giving us authority to drive out spirits in His name, just as the first disciples did. It is really very simple: We address the spirit—specifying what sort of spirit it is if we know (although this is not always necessary)—and command it to leave in the name of Jesus Christ.

The fact that the spirit does not always leave immediately reminds us that this is a spiritual battle between two kingdoms. It is indeed a power struggle. We need to know, therefore, where our resources in Christ are to be found, and how to draw upon the authority and power that are available to us. We also need to understand the reasons why spirits do not leave when commanded to do so.

The Importance of Right Theology

The spiritual battle involved in deliverance has many aspects. At the heart of it all is faith, a firm trust in God, that opens the way for God to work His blessings in our lives.

We can earn none of God's gifts. They must be received in faith and gratitude. And faith in God is nourished by taking in the truth about God. John writes, "You will know the truth, and the truth will set you free" (John 8:32). It is important to be sure of the truth if the battles of deliverance are to be won.

God and Satan

Satan was previously one of God's angels. But when he rebelled, he was thrown down to earth and his angels with him. His authority in heaven was removed, but he has been allowed power on earth for a time to lead the world astray

49

(Revelation 12:7–9, 17). Eventually Satan and his angels will be thrown into the "eternal fire" where "they will be tormented day and night for ever and ever" (Matthew 25:41; Revelation 20:10).

Fallen Humanity

The first human beings, Adam and Eve, gave authority to the serpent by believing him and doubting God (Genesis 3:1–19). In so doing they put themselves in subservience to Satan, since the serpent is Satan (Revelation 12:9).

These passages from Genesis, even without a literal reading, describe the truth of how human sin has enabled Satan's present hold in the world. Human beings lost their dominion over the earth, so childbearing, relationships between men and women, and working the earth all became riddled with pain and struggle (Genesis 1:26; 3:16–19).

Jesus

Jesus was born and died completely sinless (Hebrews 4:15). His perfect obedience to God put Him in a victorious position over Satan, not under him. He came as the Second Adam, the pioneer of restored human beings. The demons recognized Him as "the Holy One of God," because they knew He had authority in Himself to destroy them (Mark 1:24).

Jesus cast out evil spirits with His own authority. This was quite different from anything that had taken place before, and it caused the crowds to gasp (Mark 1:27).

Through His obedient death on the cross, Jesus offered the perfect sacrifice for sin. He stood in the place of sinful human beings under God's judgment. Satan cannot bring any valid accusations against those who trust in Jesus' sacrificial death. "Now the prince of this world will be driven out," Jesus said as He approached the cross (John 12:31).

This same victory of Jesus over the powers of darkness that are set against us is clear in Paul's letter to the Colossians:

> God made you alive with Christ. He forgave us all our sins, having cancelled the written code, with all its regulations, that was against us and that stood opposed to us; he took it away, nailing it to the cross. And having disarmed the powers and

authorities, he made a public spectacle of them, triumphing over them by the cross.

Colossians 2:13–15

When God raised Jesus from the dead, He clearly proved Him to be the Messiah, the Ruler over sin and death. All who believe in Him through faith now share in His divine life.

The People of the New Order

The Messiah was long promised as the One whom God would send to set His people free from sin. Israel's calling to bring blessings to the whole world has been fulfilled in Jesus and His people.

Through faith in Jesus, believers now have authority to proclaim the Good News and, in His name, to heal the sick and cast out evil spirits. The age of resurrection has begun. Death no longer rules us; instead there is divine life found in Christ. For the people of Jesus, eternity is certain. The presence of the Holy Spirit with us now is a "down payment" of what will one day be our full inheritance with Christ in heaven.

God must complete His purposes so that sin and evil are completely destroyed. The return of Christ and the final Day of the Lord are certain. The Kingdom of God will come. The new creation will be complete.

As the Church, the people of Christ, witness to the ultimate purpose of God, the ministries of healing and deliverance are signs of what is to come; and they are clear expressions of God's compassion in the here and now.

Christian believers are God's priesthood. Linking earth and heaven, we are called to be channels through whom God's Kingdom blessings flow freely to His world.

A Biblical Example of Deliverance

They went to Capernaum, and when the Sabbath came, Jesus went into the synagogue and began to teach. The people were amazed at his teaching, because he taught them as one who had authority, not as the teachers of the law. Just then a man in their synagogue who was possessed by an evil spirit cried out, "What do you want with us, Jesus of Nazareth? Have you come to destroy us? I know who you are—the Holy One of God!"

"Be quiet!" said Jesus sternly. "Come out of him!" The evil spirit shook the man violently and came out of him with a shriek.

The people were all so amazed that they asked each other, "What is this? A new teaching—and with authority! He even gives orders to evil spirits and they obey him." News about him spread quickly over the whole region of Galilee.

Mark 1:21–28

Reference has been made several times in this book to Mark's account of the deliverance of the man in the synagogue. This passage is particularly instructive for approaching prayer for deliverance. Here are some significant points to note:

- As stated earlier, while many translations use the strong phrase, "a man **possessed by** an evil spirit," the Greek is more accurately translated as "a man **with** an unclean spirit," or even "a man **in** an unclean spirit" (see verse 23, emphasis added).

- Both singular and plural words are used to describe the spirit(s). "Have you come to destroy us? I know who you are" (verse 24). This indicates several spirits, but one that was in charge.

- The spirit started the contest, using Jesus' name, "the Holy One" (verse 24), to try to gain power over Jesus.

- Jesus had indeed come to destroy them. He said, "Be quiet!", or more literally, "Be throttled!" (verse 25). Then He said, "Come out of him!" (verse 25). The spirit was not sent to any particular place in this instance, but eventually it will be sent to the eternal fire.

- Jesus simply casts the evil spirit out. There was noise and some dramatic manifestations, but there was also an evangelistic impact as the news of Jesus' power and authority spread rapidly through the region.

Principal Keys to Effective Deliverance

Be Filled with the Holy Spirit's Power

Since deliverance is a power struggle, we need not only to know the authority we have been given by Christ, but also to realize that the power of God can move through us. God's authority is fixed and given, in principle, to all Christians, since all are disciples. (Individual churches, however, have their own patterns for authorizing ministry that need to be respected.) The power of God, on the other hand, varies in its presence, and we must learn to seek it.

Jesus gave His followers both power and authority to do this ministry of deliverance as they traveled through the country proclaiming the Kingdom of God (Luke 9:1). Powerful deliverance ministry flows from a powerful prayer life. Some spirits only come out after much prayer and, perhaps, fasting (Mark 9:29).

Discern the Evil Spirit's "Right" to Be There and Deal with the Sin That Gives It That Right

A vital factor in driving out evil spirits is to address what gives them their "right" to be there in the first place. Satan has no authority in the lives of those who are God's, except where sin has not been confessed and dealt with.

Where sin has allowed a foothold, this must be confessed in the presence of another Christian (James 5:16). Often there is reluctance to do this because of shame about a particular sin; common examples of this include sexual acts outside marriage, lustful acts or unforgiveness toward another person. The way forward may be private confession to someone in the team of the same sex before the deliverance prayer goes ahead.

This point indicates the importance of working in teams that include both men and women. Deliverance ministry should not usually be attempted on one's own; having someone else present provides protection both physically and as a witness to what is said and done. With more powerful spirits an even larger team is advisable.

As described in chapter 4, the sin that gives the spirit the right to be present may be primarily voluntary—of the person's own will. Alternatively, it may be involuntary, originating in a person's ancestors or in the sin of some other person toward the person concerned. Sometimes people have great difficulty speaking of the hurt or abuse caused to them. They need to be assured that the intent is not to blame them but only to bring the truth to light. Where there is truth, there may be full forgiveness expressed and the spirit can be identified and driven out. Even still, there are times in which the pain is so great that it has to be unfolded gradually.

More difficult to remove are the spirits passed down that relate to sins from several generations back. A complex weave of sins can be built up over several generations, and this can cause multiple spirit presence. The nature of the spirits will be seen in the problems encountered by the person, but not always very clearly, and what originally gave them right of entry into the family line is not always easy to discover.

It is helpful, and sometimes essential, to receive knowledge directly from God about the sin at the point of entry. Every church seeking to practice deliverance ministry therefore needs to learn to receive through the Holy Spirit what are called "words of knowledge" or a "message of knowledge" (1 Corinthians 12:8). One example of Jesus' using such a word of knowledge is found in John 4:18.

In my experience, over the course of time some team members learn to hear remarkable words of knowledge very accurately. However, great care and wisdom need to be exercised until such words are confirmed, lest damage be done; for example, by inappropriately putting a slur on a family's reputation.

If there is difficulty in discerning the point of entry of a spirit, it may be necessary to return to the ministry on another occasion after further prayer. Some deliverance ministry takes time and several sessions. God honors our perseverance and leads us step by step. There is no shortcut to learning other than by experience.

In Preparation for Deliverance, the People Seeking Ministry Should:

- Confess all known personal sins and ask for God's forgiveness.

- Renounce all occult involvement—either their own or their ancestors'—including any possible witchcraft, Satanism or Freemasonry.

- Ask God to have mercy on those in previous generations who gave Satan the opportunity to enter through sin, acknowledging that we, too, are sinners.

- Speak forgiveness to all who have caused hurt and against whom bitterness, resentment or hatred have been harbored. This should also be toward ancestors for actions that caused spiritual bondage even to the present day. It is important to speak words blessing those who did wrong (Luke 6:28; Romans 12:14).

- Confess Jesus Christ as the Son of God, and their personal Savior from sin. Declare that Jesus Christ is made Lord over every aspect of their lives. This is the supreme goal for every believer's life and the key to complete deliverance from the enemy's hold.

- Renounce any spirit believed to be present.

- Pray a prayer of protection, if appropriate.

- Command the spirit to leave in Jesus' name.

The ground of victory lies solely in what Jesus has accomplished. It is powerful to proclaim this confidently as the ministry proceeds. The words used in prayer should stress the following:

- the sinlessness of Jesus, the Holy One

- the sacrificial work of Jesus on the cross; His blood that dealt with sin and thereby destroyed the accuser's weapons

- the name of Jesus—to which every knee will bow

- the Kingdom or rule of God that Jesus has established

- God's praise, which effectively expresses God's rule and therefore overthrows the rule of the enemy; Satan and his spirits hate the worship of God

It is important that one person is in charge of the prayer, even if the authority is passed to others at certain times. Team members should respect the leader's authority.

Remind the demon of the authority you have in Jesus Christ and command it to leave in the name of Jesus. Frequently, but not always, there will be at least mild manifestations in the person's body; these may be signs of a struggle or of a spirit leaving. Coughing is common, and vomiting occurs on occasion.

Most spirits leave through the mouth, while some leave in the way they came, for example, through the eyes, the sexual orifices or the fingers. They hold on to parts of the body (the person being set free is often aware of this), but this hold can be released in Jesus' name. It is important to remember that the spirits are deceptive and may appear to have gone when they have not.

Deliverance does not need noise; it needs faith in God, in the authority He has committed to us and in the power of the Spirit. I tend to raise my voice a bit in order to bolster my confidence as I command the intruder to leave. But noise is not necessary and can be distracting, frightening or simply a sign that our faith is weak. If we want deliverance ministry to be treated as routine and undramatic, we need to be as matter-of-fact and quietly firm about it as possible.

It can be helpful to command the spirits to neither hurt anyone nor make a noise. The release of deep emotional pain, however, can easily be confused with the cries of a spirit.

On occasion it is better not to use words like *demon* or *spirit.* Our team ministered to a Christian who also told fortunes. She was quite unable to cope with the notion that evil spirits were operating in her. "I am a good person," she insisted. More judicious words should have been used by the team. If there was confession and repentance, probably a quiet prayer to send any darkness or power away would have been sufficient. A lot of deliverance happens without mention of the word *spirits!*

The person seeking deliverance should be encouraged to be an active participant in expelling the spirit. Calling on Jesus for help may be necessary. It can also be helpful to breathe in the Holy Spirit—taking in a deep breath with the intention of receiving the Spirit, then expelling the demon, coughing and breathing it out.

No method should be used that violates the dignity of the person. Long and protracted sessions should also be avoided: There should be appropriate breaks for drink or rest.

At the end of the ministry time, the place that was previously occupied by the evil spirits must be filled with the Holy Spirit, usually with laying on of hands. I commit the person to God's care, asking that, where further ministry is needed, the

Holy Spirit will prepare the person, bringing to light what needs to be known.

"How Do You Know When the Spirits Have Gone?"

You may not always know; sometimes you have to believe this by faith. In due course it becomes clear if the problem the spirits created is gone. Often, however, the person knows that the spirit has gone, the manifestations cease or you yourself know inwardly.

Some say that demons should be sent to the lake of fire or to report to Jesus. I am content just to command them to depart, as Jesus did. As Twelftree shows, Jesus understood deliverance to be in two stages: At the first stage the demon leaves the person, and at the second the final defeat of Satan and his demons takes place at the last judgment.[1] Since all demons will go ultimately to the "lake of fire" (Matthew 25:41; Revelation 20:10), it does no harm to remind them of this fact.

When spirits do not leave in response to our commands it is best to avoid prolonging the ministry by endlessly repeating what you have already done. Instead look further for:

- Occult practices that have not been confessed, renounced and dealt with
- Sin that has not been confessed, or if confessed, not truly repented of
- Sin by ancestors (A family tree may be helpful to indicate patterns of disorder or death in unnatural circumstances; words of knowledge may be needed to fully determine these.)
- Lack of will to be set free
- Lack of faith that Christ has brought about complete freedom
- An unhealthy bond to a person (possibly a dead person)
- The possibility of an incorrect diagnosis—the problem may not lie with a spirit at all

Further prayer, listening to God and perhaps fasting may be called for. In *Christian, Set Yourself Free,* Graham Powell describes how after many years of torment his own deliverance came through believing that Christ had set him free from the evil spirits in him. He then took authority over them, commanding them to go in the name of Christ. Many times before this, well-meaning Christian ministers, after failing to accomplish the deliverance, had told him that there were no evil spirits in him.[2]

I have found personally that the effectiveness of my prayers for deliverance has increased as two convictions have deepened within me: the first, **the immense power of the Holy Spirit;** the second, **a holy anger at the presence of such intruders in the lives of God's created people.**

Pray for Protection If Necessary

Most people are fearful when first setting out in this ministry, and a prayer of protection is wise. I have found the following prayer to be helpful: "We claim the protection of the blood of Jesus over each person here, our families, our church families and over all the possessions God has given us to steward."

Jesus has transferred us from the kingdom of darkness to His own Kingdom (Colossians 1:13), and we are secure and fully protected in Him. There is nothing to fear, as He repeatedly told His disciples. We are completely loved by God and have been given authority for this ministry. When we are sure of our standing in Christ, we will not find it so necessary to ask specially for protection; indeed, quite a lot of concern to do this comes from fear rather than from faith. Although fear is understandable, it is nevertheless not God's best for us, and it gives Satan opportunity. While the prayer of protection guards against this, it is better still not to be afraid.

The Importance of Working under Authority

One of the problems in the Church of England is that prayer for deliverance is not yet accepted as routine prayer. The presence of evil spirits is treated as a rare phenomenon requiring great caution. In many dioceses no deliverance ministry is to be attempted without reference to the bishop or whomever he designates. This is impractical if spirits are widespread and mostly not very powerful (such as those I earlier described having picked up).

In *Deliverance,* Michael Perry draws a distinction between a lesser exorcism, or prayers asking for deliverance, and a greater exorcism involving a direct command to the demon or demonic forces. He argues that only for the greater exorcism is the bishop's permission necessary.[3] This seems unsatisfactory, however, if Jesus is our model, since He dealt with all spirits by command.

If you work in a church such as in the Anglican or Roman Catholic faiths, where you are under wider authority, I suggest you seek an agreement with your bishop that you consult with him only over any case that looks serious and has the feel of a major deliverance about it. Nevertheless, in handling the smaller stuff locally, you and other members of your team must work under a careful authority structure in the local church.

In conclusion, it is important that anyone who practices the ministry of deliverance should do so under the proper authority of his or her minister, who should be under the proper authority established in that church.

Study questions:

1. What do we need to understand theologically in order to combat evil in Jesus' name?
2. What are the keys to driving out evil spirits?
3. How should a person prepare for receiving deliverance ministry?
4. How do we know whether or not a spirit has left?
5. Is this ministry something in which you can engage under the authority of your local church?

Notes

1. Graham Twelftree, *Christ Triumphant: Exorcism Then and Now* (London: Hodder and Stoughton, 1984), p. 102.
2. Graham Powell, *Christian, Set Yourself Free* (Tonbridge, England: Sovereign World, 1994), p. 12.
3. Michael Perry, *Deliverance* (London: SPCK, 1987), p. 143.

7

After Deliverance

It cannot be emphasized too strongly that the purpose of deliverance ministry is to help people, not to cast out spirits. God is looking for believers who have a firm faith in Christ and hold to His promises; He is looking for a resolute will to choose good thoughts and actions; He is looking for people who, within the fellowship of the Church, will obey Him and move in the power of the Holy Spirit. The ministry of deliverance has its place, but it is only one part in the much greater context of Christian growth and ministry.

When a person's will is weak, or his or her faith shallow, deliverance will be difficult to sustain. It requires good soil to resist sin and Satan and for the Word of Christ to bear fruit. In many cases, much work has to be done before deliverance will be complete—work to build good foundations of faith in Christ and a resolute will.

Rebuilding the Will
Some people will return again and again for deliverance, when what they really need is discipline in their thoughts, aligning their minds with Scripture and choosing to believe what God says is true and not what their feelings are saying. In the more complex cases, a successful deliverance ministry will proceed step by step with a program of faith building in the person. This may happen through fellowship groups in the church, personal study of the Bible, prayer or one-on-one nurture by experienced leaders.

The rebuilding of the will in weak-natured people is a much more difficult task than the prayer for deliverance. It involves helping people set manageable goals which they can achieve, thereby giving them confidence. As they grow, their targets can become more stretching. Only when the will becomes strong can people possibly choose for themselves the right attitudes and actions necessary to resist Satan. Living in a supportive community will help.

It is helpful to teach those receiving deliverance ministry to move forward in the following ways:

1. **Accept firmly that as believers who are "in Christ," they are secure and protected.** Satan cannot harm them.

2. **Be strongly on guard against any temptation to sin,** especially in thoughts of self-rejection or self-hatred, or of unforgiveness or anger towards others.

3. **Stick closely to other Christians** while the old patterns of thoughts or actions are being broken.

4. **Learn Scripture** and use it to combat the lies that Satan feeds into their thoughts.

5. **When the conflict is strong, call upon Jesus for help** and for the Holy Spirit's presence to fill them daily.

6. **Drive Satan away with words such as these:** "In the name of Jesus, go from me, Satan. I serve Jesus as Lord and belong to Him."

Following deliverance ministry, people may well feel tired and weak. They may even feel the loss of their former identities as people, if the spirits had pressed in hard on their attitudes and personalities. It will take time for them to find their new identities as the people God intended them to be. It is important to support them with plenty of love and help in this period and to let their stability develop before they are asked to share their testimonies.

Answers to Questions about This Ministry

Since the ministry of deliverance from evil spirits is foreign to our Western culture, it is not surprising that it easily arouses concern. I believe that all questions regarding this ministry need to be considered carefully. I hope that throughout this book many legitimate objections have been clarified by my explanations. I offer in addition my response to three further common grounds for concern.

1. "Belief in evil spirits is a way of evading personal responsibility for evil."

Experience in this ministry soon bears out that people only become free of evil spirits when they take full responsibility and with all their strength of will turn away from what is wrong. In no way is full personal responsibility sidestepped. It is sin alone that gives Satan's spirits any right to be present; deliverance therefore requires firm repentance as well as confession and forgiveness. Work is often necessary to help someone face this responsibility before deliverance can be both accomplished and sustained.

2. "Belief in evil spirits fosters a superstitious, primitive approach to the world."

Most of the world is convinced that evil spirits exist, and we in Western cultures need to be open to the possibility that this view is accurate. With correct teaching, this attitude can be handled quite factually and without creating an aura of superstition.

A belief in evil spirits need not be in conflict with the truths discovered in psychology or medicine, because the explanations offered on each side are not necessarily mutually exclusive. They can be complementary. Believing that someone has a demon does not mean believing that he or she does not need psychiatric help. I look forward to future constructive participation in working together for people's health.

3. "Deliverance ministry is dangerous and can be followed by suicide or violent crime."

Wherever people are under professional care for their condition, as a rule I always work in consultation with their psychiatrists, physicians, counselors or social workers. It is important not to disrupt the existing pattern of treatment. Furthermore, one mistake in the ministry of deliverance can lead to justified condemnation for a ministry that is often seen as unprofessional.

When people are under professional psychiatric care, their personality is often seriously disturbed and is not capable of providing a firm basis for the repentance and faith that is necessary for effective deliverance. In this sort of case, it may not be appropriate to proceed at all with deliverance ministry. But when proceeding, certainly it is vital to do so with great caution, and remain in the bounds of the partnership I have already emphasized.

If deliverance ministry with more stable people is practiced under firm leadership and authority in the local church, it will ensure that potentially difficult cases are treated responsibly and with wisdom. During my time as the vicar of Holy Trinity Church in Coventry, England, two doctors were members of our ministry team, and we consistently involved them in such cases.

Praying the Kingdom

One prayer that can be prayed at any time is simply, "Your Kingdom come, Lord, in my friend." The Kingdom of God is His rule of order, wholeness and love. It is how Jesus taught us to pray. We can pray God's Kingdom into any person, institution, nation or church: "Your Kingdom come. Your will be done on earth, as in heaven." This prayer will prepare the ground for possible healing and deliverance ministry later.

Study questions:

1. What does the author mean by saying "the purpose of deliverance is to help people, not to cast out spirits"?
2. Why is deliverance difficult to sustain when a person's will is weak or his or her faith is shallow?
3. How do we teach those who are receiving ministry to move forward in their deliverance?
4. Have you encountered any of the concerns listed in this chapter? Do you know how to answer them?
5. Are you "praying the Kingdom" into the lives of the people around you?

Bishop Graham Dow is a graduate of Nottingham University, Birmingham University and Clifton Theological College. Ordained a priest in 1968, he served as the vicar of Holy Trinity Church in Coventry, England, from 1982 to 1992; the canon theologian of Coventry Cathedral from 1988 to 1992; and the Area Bishop of Willesden from 1992 to 2000.

Dow is the author of many books, including *Pathways of Prayer, A Christian Understanding of Daily Work* and *Christian Renewal in Europe.* He and his wife, Molly, have four children.